T0154461

The Alchemist's Kitchen

Books by Susan Rich

The Cartographer's Tongue / Poems of the World (2000)

Cures Include Travel (2006)

The Alchemist's Kitchen

poems

Susan Rich

WHITE PINE PRESS / BUFFALO, NEW YORK

White Pine Press
P.O. Box 236, Buffalo, New York 14201
www.whitepine.org

Acknowledgments to the following journals where these poems first appeared,
often in an earlier version. Sincere thanks to the editors for their belief in my work.
Antioch Review, "The Never Born Comes of Age," *Art Access*, "Corner of My Studio,"
"Unexpected Song," *Barn Owl Review*, "Tender," *Bellevue Literary Review*,
"Transcendence," *Cold Mountain Review*, "Awaiting Further Instruction," *Crab Creek
Review*, "Not a Still Life," *Cimarron Review*, "Day of the Disquieted Heart," *5 AM*,
"Chanterelle," *Diode*, "The 4 O'Clock News @ House of Sky," *Florida Review*, "For
My Student Who Would Prefer to Remain Anonymous," *The Gettysburg Review*, "Re-
Imagining My Life with Lions," *Good Times - Santa Cruz*, "What the Grocer Knows,"
Green Mountains Review, "Day of the Global Heart," *Harvard Review*, "Interview,"
Margie, "An Army of Ellipses Traveling Over All She Does Not Say ...," *Iota Journal*,
"Turning 50 with a Line from Robert Hayden," *New England Review*, "At Middle
Life: A Romance," *Notre Dame Review*, "Tulip Sutra," *New Orleans Review*, "What Do
You Remember from Before the War ...," *New South Review*, "Day of the Insatiable
Heart," *Northwest Review*, "The [In] Visible Architecture of Existence," *Poetry
International*, "Food for Fallen Angels," "The Usual Mistakes," *Poetry Ireland Review*,
"Entering the Abandoned Red Barn: Old Photograph," *Rattle*, "Daphne Swears
Off It," *Redheaded Stepchild*, "Doing Time," *The Southern Review*, "Mr. Myra Albert
Wiggins Recalls Their Arrangement," "Cruise of the Christians," *Third Coast*,
"Hunger is the Best Cook," *Times Literary Supplement* (London), "Different Places to
Pray," *TriQuarterly*, "Art Lessons," "Letter to the End of the Year," *Valparaiso Poetry
Review*, "You Might Consider," "Aperture," *Women's Review of Books*, "Curating My
Death," "What to Make of Such Beauty."
    Thanks to the following anthologies:
Poets of the American West, MT: Many Voices Press, 2010, "Naming It,".

First Edition

Cover image: Philipp Schumacher

Printed and bound in the United States of America

ISBN 978-1-935210-14-6

Library of Congress Control Number: 2009937823

A thousand and one thank yous to my community of South Grand Poets who continue to care for and sustain me. I am more grateful than I can express for their sound critique, fine wine, and fabulous laughter: T. Clear, Jeff Crandall, Kathleen Flenniken, Kathyrn Hunt, Rosanne Olson, Ted McMahon, Peter Pereira, and Gary Winans.

For giving their time and expertise for close readings and critiques of this book, I am forever thankful to Kelli Russell Agodon, Kathleen Flenniken and Mary Peelen.

Heartfelt thanks to Northwest poets Peter Aaron, Allen Braden, Nancy Canyon, Joseph Green, Katelyn Hibbard, Jenifer Lawrence, and for a generosity of spirit and insight that support my belief that poets can change the world. Thank you to Christine Devall and John Marshall for creating and sustaining Open Books Poetry Emporium — a sanctuary for poets as well as poetry.

A deep bow to the Breakfast Club of Tommy Kim, Monica Lemoine, Matt Schwisow, and Ben Thomas for sustenance of all kinds.

Forever thanks to Kissley Leonor and Jeremiah Sasson Fryer for Almeria.

Thank you also to the organizations and foundations that have supported the creation of this work: Artists Trust for a GAP Grant supporting travel to Bosnia and Herzegovina and professional development leave from Highline Community College that allowed for many of these poems to come into being. A heartfelt thanks to 4Culture for an award allowing for continued work on the photography of Myra Albert Wiggins.

Thanks to the founders, directors, and staff, of the following artist residencies and foundations: Fundacion Valparaiso, Hedgebrook, Helene Whitely Center, and the Ucross Foundation.

Thank you B. Ruby Rich and Mary Peelen for love, support, friendship and family — all offered with grace and gorgeous food.

And to Dennis Maloney and Elaine LaMattina, the awesome alchemists behind White Pine Press: thank you, thank you, thank you.

"They are the proof that something was there and no longer is. Like a stain. And the stillness of them is boggling. You can turn away but when you come back they'll still be there looking at you."

—Diane Arbus

Table of Contents

INCANTATION

TRANSFORMATION

Song

Incantation

Different Places to Pray

Everywhere, everywhere she wrote; something is falling —
a ring of keys slips out of her pocket into the ravine below;

nickels and dimes and to do lists; duck feathers from a gold pillow.
Everywhere someone is losing a favorite sock or a clock stops

circling the day; everywhere she goes she follows the ghost
of her heart; jettisons everything but the shepherd moon.

This is the way a life unfolds: decoding messages from profiteroles,
the weight of mature plums in late autumn. She'd prefer a compass

rose, a star chart, text support messages delivered from the net,
even the local pet shop — as long as some god rolls away the gloss

and grime of our gutted days, our global positioning crimes.
Tell me, where do you go to pray — a river valley, a pastry tray?

Food for Fallen Angels

If food be the music of love, play on —
Twelfth Night, misremembered

If they can remember living at all, it is the food they miss:
a plate of goji berries, pickled ginger, gorgonzola prawns
dressed on a bed of miniature thyme, a spoon

glistening with pomegranate seeds, Russian black bread
lavished with July cherries so sweet, it was dangerous to revive;
to slide slowly above the lips, flick and swallow, almost . . .

Perhaps more like this summer night: lobsters in the lemon grove
a picnicker's trick of moonlight and platters; the table dressed
in gold kissed glass, napkins spread smooth as dark chocolate.

If they sample a pastry — glazed Florentine, praline heart —
heaven is lost. It's the cinnamon and salt our souls return for —
rocket on the tongue, the clove of garlic: fresh and flirtatious.

Tulip Sutra

> The letters that make up "lale," the Turkish word for "tulip," are the same as those that form Allah."
>
> — from *Tulipomania*

Praise the origin
of the frilled double latte:

lofty wild flowers on a rocky ledge.

Praise tulips from Turkey,
tulips from China,

tulips born in Afghanistan —

✻

Praise the turbulence
of desire tucked inside

this hobo flower

glimpsed along highways —
small pink vases —

transforming evenings
into reckless weekends.

✻

Before the flowers
depart the harbor, bless

one Istanbul merchant

as he scatters his gift
into bolts of bottle-blue cloth —

praise this small token:

tulips for a foreign friend.

*

And the Flemish merchant
who opens the crates

mistakes the bulbs for coarse, funny onions

seasons them
in vinegar-mint —

but keeps a handful back for his garden —

remember him.

*

How not to believe
in a flower which honors lips

in its names:

Increaser of Pleasure,
Rose of the Dawn,
My Light of Paradise —

Bless each blossom that opens and opens

traveling beyond itself

as it flutters, disheveled
by the bedroom door.

                    *

Dutch tulips succeeded
in breeding

with tulips coming
from Crete, from Kurdistan;

this intermingling is key

to the Netherlands historical
oligarchy.

                    *

In spring, bless the farmers of Skagit,
who plant acre upon acre

the tractors, the hands
that nurture each offset

until the lyric flares —

into tulips of feather, of flame.

*

And yes to a tapestry
shielding man from misfortune

more precious than song or sword;

the Sultan's son saved —
by a constellation of tulips

embroidered into his underclothes.

Bless the thread that connects
us to him.

*

Praise the curious tourist
appearing late April

despite winds, and rain, and muck —

who finds her way
by the edge of lit fields —

to witness in one
collusion of color

the return of tulips in flight —

the morning sky
upstaged by a blaze of delight.

Re-Imagining My Life with Lions

There is no death, only a change of worlds
— Marmoud Darwish

Like the unexpected glow —

small fringed shawls of witch hazel
contradict the spell of winter;

I want to live another life —

a poplar tree in a row
of blue pine along a cobbled road;

or a pomegranate

opening out, at last

over a lake of Mediterranean light.

Each day unfurls, fragrant
as a botanist's notes from the road.

I'm ready to travel someday
soon to the other side —

to visit with my cousin, gone —

three months; to gaze
into the wonder of deceased eyes.

Instead, I feed the black
bamboo, orbit the alstroemeria,

glitter over seawater at low tide.

The 4 0' Clock News @ House of Sky

In the beginning, we wanted

to cast ourselves
as opera stars, to break apart

like gorgeous women
palm reading at the piano bar —

music stinging like salt from the sea.

We were spiraling ridges, dust-darlings
and dangerous.

We were peonies — cut
and arranged like astronauts

in flight. We soaked in syllables

not water; rode the Southern
drawl of the wind

over cobalt glass —
backlit by a disc of sun.

What Do You Remember from Before the War?

Srebrenica, Bosnia, the world's first United Nations Safe Area, was the site of the worst case of genocide in Europe since World War II. In July 1995, over a period of five days, the Bosnian Serb soldiers systematically murdered over 7,000 men and boys in fields, schools, and warehouses.

— *Srebrenica: A Cry from the Grave*

In the summer there was always music
as we wandered Srebrenica's gardens
the Eyes of Beautiful Water moving like mystics.

Suitors offered tulips, Italian lipsticks.
We'd kiss and tell, comparing different men.
In the summer there was always music

as we made love, our magic word spelled *picnic*
in fields, forests, waterfalls and often
the Eyes of Beautiful Water waving like mystics.

Cleansing our faces in those fountains lit
our so-called spirits, forged a passageway within.
In the summer there was always music.

So that July, when the news turned cryptic
we'd meet at midnight, tango limb to limb.
The Eyes of Beautiful Water flowing like mystics.

We hoarded joy, each day more surrealistic —
massacres, guns, Serb mortars and violins.
In the summer there was always music.
The Eyes of Beautiful Water disappearing like mystics.

Facing 50 with a Line by Robert Hayden

There is so much that clings to us —
not just cat fur and grass

seed, but also chocolate

creams and the white beach
of childhood, an extended sash of blue.

        ✻

Not just sadness and solace,

but what the body
reveals after waking,

the open heart and a watery

sense of who we are, the life we attempt to choose.

        ✻

What clings to us (train trips, questions)
fall forward to all

the future will randomly

produce in an email, an hour,
a knot of pleasure — nearly pursued.

        ✻

The seasons clock on

redecorating the light we crave
like a dim-sum tray —

rich, sensual, and brand new

to each other —

     ✿

as Shakespearean fools, as Pomeranians,

a bright pair of trusted boots.

Tender

She will be known as the Michelangelo
of the Golden Kimono

the magician of the Singapore Sling.

On Sundays, half insane with a feeling
she can't name

she opens a bottle of absinthe, breathes in

the bitter sting of a Lancashire spring
and thinks how a tender-leafed herb

begat an international outlaw;

how the wonder of swizzles, juleps, and flips,
could bring her here, to this.

Behind the bar's immaculate boundary line —

her fingertips linger
around a jigger, a beak, a shaker, a flask —

she exchanges Polynesian parasols
for yellow sugar pistols, relinquishes

a lobster stick for one elliptical orange twist.

Toward evening's end
she'll pour herself a pony of Calvados,

add an unmeasured dash
of Caribbean grenadine,

conjuring her own blue mix.

And in the moment of last orders
she will shake her customers, stir them

to a momentary bliss
with a Devil's Whisker, a rhythmic Widow's Kiss.

An Army of Ellipses Traveling
Over All She Does Not Say...

When the war began ...
my mother baked nothing

but biscuits. Basket after basket

so big — she carried with us —
a new kind of picnic ...

Translated, she knew
it meant: the next eight days

we would eat...

✳ ✳ ✳

In Nairobi, we tried to live...
not like refugees

until the police picked up my sister ...

booked her at the station
because she looks Somali.

Afterwards ...

when father came ...
found ... dollars for the bribes...

later, after midnight,
I traveled alone to the next new country ...

* * *

By the open window of the bus …
near me … one woman

lost her bracelets, and her wrist

to the handiwork of bandits.
I think he might have seen …

something expensive …

in the day's broken light
three glass bangles …

taunting him like a god.

Cereal Boxes

Globalized in seven languages
even breakfast becomes a souvenir
of the surreal; Roman or Cyrillic,
heated milk or cold. The morning

rain takes aim with such brutality
of sound it's like a Sarajevo Rose.
And in the pre-dawn hour, who
can say — sniper fire or the idiosyncratic

lightning of a thunder bolt?
Apartment dwellers eye the backstairs,
their oven-proof plastic bowls — then help
themselves to seconds of *Chex*, of *Cheerios*.

Day of the Global Heart

The way of the heart
is that it shifts —

speaks in lace,
in blood red phrases:

holocausts, amphetamines,
Arctic glaciers.

The way of the heart
is to cry out

broadcast, abhor —
Srebrenica and Katrina —

our Iraq war —
then beat by beat

ignore, ignore, ignore.

The selfish heart —
that hypocritical tart

hides her actions
and erasures

like the infant
she forsook at birth

which one day returns —
face shorn, heart

spectral, demanding
reparations:

a pound of flesh —
extracted, salted, cured —

our failures historical
our heartlessness beyond words.

Paradise Now *at Highline Community College*

— directed by Hany Abu-Assad

The boys argue about the end, did the bomb detonate?
They can't agree. They try out multiple meanings for white

light, two human eyes, the break-neck speed of Said's life;
his grief. The black ash of question marks begin to rise

reluctantly above their freshmen heads — the procrastinated
fall into inquiry; *But what has it to do with me?*

I try out flashback, foreshadow — hope to teach the world
of mise-en-scene — to watch students interrogate

their own thinking. They side so easily with the suicide
bomber; understand instinctively two best friends

toppled by geography, their familiar junkyard lives.
In class discussion, my students appear almost dreamy —

Can there be a film industry, without a country?
Intifada and *Mossad* lift off their tongues

with hard-won confidence; the glossary — their global gun.
On which edge of the checkpoint do they rely? Arab

or Israeli? The questions with new answers lead them on,
keep them fractured, shiftshape some through to another side.

For My Student,
Who Would Prefer to Remain Anonymous

What do you like to do outside of school? In what are you an expert?

On the first day of the quarter
she admits her talent for turning invisible.
And in the left hand corner of a tunnel shaped room
there's no need to elaborate —
She dips down behind the last grey desk
eyes blinking as if to stave off
encroaching student orchestrations
and becomes a click of buttons, a camel
colored coat, frayed carpet bag.
With the build of a discus thrower
she's a maple skinned Olympian.
I imagine her inside a magician's box
cloaked in velveteen and mourning doves
and want to tell her there's no reason
to disappear from Contemporary World Literature,
from novels of India and Egypt
where women refuse to take *no* for an answer.
As class continues four days a week at noon
she begins to speak in a wisp of a voice,
insight delivered between uncertain pauses
in almost inaudible tones.
Three times she disappears from class:
       diet pills mixed with Dramamine
       an auntie's death
       finally, she's hit by a truck
       crossing as the sign says, *Walk.*
And today, although she's my first thought
in the morning, I've almost forgotten her face.

Havielle: her expertise nearly coming true.
I'd like to find her, say *I know*
what it's like to want to disappear
until no one notices you at all.
A ghost that plays in empty rooms,
preferable to an open wrist, an accidental slip.

Portrait with Lorca

Beneath her shirt, pages are turning,
climbing her shoulders; images
rearranging her breasts, the thin line

of clavicle — highlighting her underwire
x: two satin cups, black straps. Beneath her
shirt, lives were being lived by other men

and women. Families acquired toddlers,
several gerbils, teens. Often the world
beneath her blouse took precedence

over what happened at school.
And so, when the leather binding
touched her belly, nestled near her hips,

flirted with a reference to a Lorca aperitif ~
she could no longer fool the old professor
who had loved someone, or two.

And when the tests came back
her examination booklet marked
with almond skins, perfume, and candle wax —

the commentary simply said —
We all wear branches that we do not
have. Castanet! Castanet! Castanet!

Interview

In her mind, she needs to cross the boundary
navigate clear water, sleep again, be whole —
she'll erase her Muslim name, forget life's memory.

Why not Bavaria? Why not the travel remedy?
Study without the Sarajevo Rose.
Her mind a boat; she floats across the boundary.

Everyone said, *the conflict? only temporary* —
She'll call her family often; keep close by telephone;
pour the past away, skip the shit of memory.

But each night she pays, this is not her country.
The thoughts shoot back and forth, a mental palindrome.
Her mind: ocean without boundary.

Other students stare in disbelief as she leaves, quietly —
a homing instinct, streams; she charts the map alone.
Is the past no more than present memory?

For one moment, her return is almost celebratory.
Mortar rounds and shelling, a kind of pleasure dome.
Her mind circles round blue boundaries.

Ode to the Question of Blue

As in delphiniums at dusk,
berries, fish, and
calm lagoon;
as in the changing days —
blue ray, blue corn, blue tooth.
I tried to know you once —
blue stocking, blue collar,
blue swoon — but better to come
to you now through canopied
rooms, to enter the cornflower
sky — where I will relinquish my
indigo boots and stone-washed jeans
above a river of pine —
bluebottles, blue Miles, blue sighs.

The Idea of Ice Cream at Alki Beach

involves a responsive sweet cream text
soaked in internal summer weather;

it infuses rock salt quiet with dry heat;
the fragrance of Greek ice, whorled with fig tree honey.

The idea of ice cream may tap into pure elation —
(she licked the scoop as lovely as the sea).

A taste of dark chocolate and true pistachio
suffice for travelers from New England or Dubai.

The idea of ice cream does not diminish over time
does not sing dripping each to each

but slowly thrums toward the galactic divine —
indifferent to the tourist on the beach.

Is it time for the little truck to turn
toward the curbstone of our street?

We'd like to know. And soon.
Let's walk out and place our palms

above the silver sliding pane. Listen to
the possum as the circus tunes come near

and we dream the ancient, clear refrain
of *mine, mine, mine.* We call and calling

make it so — the sundaes, rockets, and éclairs
we hold and in holding uphold the American

ritual of joy — the tongue and all its vagrant tastes,
before we unfold the cloud-lit wrappers cone to cone.

Daphne Swears Off It

She wants to answer yes no more —
no more nuzzling of the earlobes,
tussle of breasts, slow rolling acts of the tongue.
Instead she takes another
glass of lemon water, watches
jasmine flowers unfurl into flying stars —
raspberries ripen, their cells exploding.
Though he licks each finger, sweetly
massages her hips, her inner wrists,
whistles while he works
the underwear down the backs of her knees —
she prefers the touch of sea grass —
honeysuckle and the scented
scrub rose of midsummer's eve.
What is one man compared to an ocean?
Broad shoulders to the shoreline's low cry?
She wants to tell him
that last night soaring just under
a creamy edge of quarter moon
she tasted desire, let it cool.
But instead she rubs his forehead
licks it tentatively, *if only*
you were sea salt, if only
an apricot tree.

To My Lover, Not Yet

Sure, it's hard to know just how we'll know:
the salt-spliced air
the clockless hours, the contours
of our earlobes. I've been expecting
you *toujours* — perhaps,
we will begin by fire
escape or forgotten Spanish bar,
high above the Alhambra;
In a nod of recognition
over the saddest of vegetable bins:
Church Street, Cambridge —
forget England. Keep cutting through
odd cul de sacs, across bridges,
tulip fields and over
blue forgotten gates.
Sir, may you turn out as I imagine:
flawed, flippant, and filled
with awe for this glimpse of world —
call it miraculous
or an alchemist's task;
call it comfort for all of us
where love has not yet been.

Transformation

A Corner of My Studio

— *after a painting by Myra Albert Wiggins, 1930*

Texture, as a kind of thought

        as if the canvas were discarded

and then someone reconsidered, after all,

        took the painting back

from the brink, as if

        someone fruitlessly

attempted to iron out a few cracks; review

        the dried out folds,

as if to hope a second time —

        distill a certain flourish, extra depth.

        Memory is like that;

a gilded hat, a blue glass jar;

        one single disguised bed.

Hunger is the Best Cook

— *After a photograph by Myra Albert Wiggins, 1898*

Dark bowl, small mouth, sumptuous spoon —

Whatever there is
there's not much here,

but the girl's intent —

enraptured nearly in the pause
and trick of it, the mythic

mirror of abeyance. Her body

opens toward the rim
of awe — all lick and swallow,

imagination readying the tongue.

* * *

Is art simply a hymn to reconfiguration:

Wild huckleberries,
wedge of bread, broken chaff

from the season's ripe wheat?

The museum patron
presumes the sharp taste —

believes fully in the meal

where the spoon doesn't waver —
where the girl will

never bring this moment to its end and eat —

＊ ＊ ＊

But this is not the story

of the actual:
moon-faced, well-fed,

photographer's daughter

re-clothed and then
again, for a mother's ambitious narrative.

The costume, the curtains, the fable

rise in what the woman
called *The Vermeer Style* —

deficiency reshaped for pleasure's sake.

＊ ＊ ＊

Fistfuls of wildflowers

rupture the room as she shoots

frame after frame

cajoling the unstudied studio pose.

Is her family shrapnel or daisy chain?
Wiggin's curved hand

charting the shutter: half right, half wrong —

lighting through to
the alchemist's kitchen —

Go West, Young Woman

Myra Wiggin's maternal grandmother, Almira Phelps, twenty-five, traveled from New England by ship to Oregon Country in 1839. That same year, Louis Daguerre invented the Daguerreotype.

Think
of the surf light

as Almira departs Massachusetts
for a place

no one she knows has seen ~

Think
why wouldn't she leave

pigeons, celibacy, the shallow focus
of cobblestone streets?

Conjure
Almira calm on the ship

in the salt-rain of a westward breeze.

Let her hand wave
a whorl of good-byes ~

Write —
Water silvering the sky.

Aperture

He knew the pulse of things: the circumference
of bagels, Masonic symbols, out-of-the-way

parlors for pistachio ice cream. Knew to send

Lillian "My Darling" cards, how to linger
in the happiness of a contraband Havana cigar.

He'd offer up the wooden box tattooed

with dancing girls and oceans to his youngest daughter.
Open ticket, little coffin, promise of something

older than mathematics or Persia or Kipling.

He knew fractured things: relatives
disappearing in pogroms, squirrels

in the attic, a wife of absent feeling.

Each sadness needs a street name: Alma,
Lola, Santa Maria. No, he could never

cheat, he told her; instead, collected pocket

protectors, Lincoln pennies, two basement closets
of burnt-out light bulb fodder — certain

that one day there'd be a way to reclaim

the broken, the shunned — snapped
filament of him, of me.

Not a Still Life

She was most desirous of round things —
Roman glass, the texture of the sea.
Iridescent bowls, porcelain masks, zinnia in spring.
Paint colors: cinnamon, ochre, green. Things that shine:
white apples, survival, a strand of turquoise beads.
She coveted ginger jars, wooden clogs, one husband
(sometimes months unseen), cloudscape, three katsura trees.
She'd meditate on chemistry, Chinese art, her New York
magazines — Bright stream of all she'd gleaned.
Among her skills: photography and psalms, how to mend
a heart, an evening dress, a career polished to a song.
Madeira, Algiers, Rhodes — the light different in each one.
But what she wanted most has all but disappeared.
The museum walls, the fame — the name not written here.

Mr. Myra Albert Wiggins
Recalls Their Arrangement

Maybe it was the bicycle. The way her hips
rose up and up — as if directed straight to heaven —

Like a Venus. And a banker's daughter — true.
Real original, this girl — a bicycle, a camera,

other newfangled tools. So I sent her bolts
of ribbon, overalls, and boots — anything to make her squint

her eyes and glance one day toward me — me: Fred
Wiggins of Wiggins Bazaar — 123 Commercial Street.

More of a back-up boyfriend, for someone like Myra
her family would say. Everyone knew she was in love

with her own life: bareback rides, opera singing,
and the New York *artiste* nights. But I expected

to live a little, too. And so if there were men
of Salem, Toppenish, Seattle, lovely and rich —

who snickered at our last-season suits
and sequined gowns, who hinted not infrequently —

that a husband should not be so happy
packing picture frames and mounting

photographs. Christ. They knew nothing.

Homesickness

after a photograph by Myra Albert Wiggins, 1901

We expect illumination
    but instead crawl into darkness

the girl's forsaken expression utterly wrong.

The mother, if it is her mother, staring
    beyond the camera's eye so clearly

absent, she could be thinking of masturbation

her bodice angled by longing: her cheek bruised
    by her own pained hand.

Hanging behind the child, a wall lamp half-obscured,

incidental nearly, except for the photographer's composition —
    absence configured in platinum.

Shadow courted like a hand maiden, a fine trap door —

as these two figures, turn inward to the mirrored lens
    we imagine through — Dutch dresses

donned in woman-made sorrow

                addictive as exile
from a water country

where you were never loved

and this mother — nothing —

but foreign, ill-equipped, torn.

Late Romance

She cannot save herself
from the allure of the new

the frame of formation
finding her subject

the memory made flesh in the catch of an F-stop.

She recalibrates her life —
a dress, a table, a coiled bowl;

collects Japanese paper and pools
of the pharmacist's blue

potions. Reverses
everything in the family's

dark rooms. The absent
husband to fedora —

the children to a plate of autumn fruit.

Paris Exposition, After Hours

— 1900, gelatin silver print

What unconscious life
does she recognize

in the restless quiet
of the stranger's shrines

as they reflect on and off the Seine?

In the confidence
of window frames

amid the upward wave
of the lanterned stairway

could the cloudscape change?

Watch how the street lights
jangle the quay, how

the revelers float like water ghosts
into feathered women.

Is *this* the other life?

The what if, perhaps,
might — still — glimpse —

Confidentially, she unfolds
the river path:

danger, misfits, gold —

Her quirky risk
to become unknown.

Polishing Brass

Myra Wiggins used her housekeeper, Alma Schmidt, as a subject in several of her pictorial photographs of Dutch domestic life. Schmidt wore costumes and posed in a variety of theatrical scenes. No further record of their relationship exists.

No, more a holy meditation
on surface and stain:

Madonna with Vessel.

The inland
glow of white shoulders

rivulet of vertebrae

vestige of one breath-
takingly long

and sexual arm
which grasps

the ledge
of the cauldron

as she curves onward.

*

Remember form:

nothing more

than potent omen —

pyramid of saucepan top,
overflow

of water bucket,
angle of the invisible skin —

dimpled underneath her arranged garment —

               ✜

A light-stroked body,
conflicted as rosewater, as clotted cream.

               ✜

Alma, grace of more
than poor

Our Lady of the Scullery Shimmer —

starlet of
returning questions

May I serve you?

*

Perhaps art as polish

gloss of what the photograph

pretends in voyeurism.

An aperture, a flash

of the nakedly conscious eye —

a part of and apart —

blessing identity until it blinds us.

*

Once, on a sunlit afternoon

a maidservant, an ingénue,

swept forward —

into what this moment you

in Almeria, Soho, Barcelona —

might admire, must revise —

a woman's hands: fingernails, blue.

What to Make of Such Beauty?

The attack lasted less than half an hour. Approximately 1,200,000 books and 600 sets of periodicals were destroyed.

— Kemal Bakarsic on the burning
of the Sarajevo National Library, August 1992

The next day along the streets of Sarajevo
scorched pieces of paper

fluttered like a strange snow.

Peel one scrap from the sky
call it hope and an urgent message

appears — for one moment —

a new form of God pentimento.
Turkish, Hebrew, and Bosnian texts ...

Desire lit in the arabesque of black, besotted alphabets —

until the warmth of the lines
recede and the magic letters fall like trash ~

fingers chalked in the floating literatures of grief.

Yet, the hardest part, Lejla says
is to not live within such burning,

not breathe in the pages of our indestructible history.

The Usual Mistakes

If the conflict lasts more than three months

you should expect problems with hips and knees —
surgeries, fireworks, friends

all of your relationships ...

He discusses the war as casually
as he reviews the football scores,

or his daughter's coincidental green card.

Before the war I never coughed, he said —
now instead of summers by the sea,

I vacation at hospital in Germany.

The body remembers
he tells me;

the body is trouble, he makes me repeat.

The Hospital Room in a City Where I Am Not

On the last day

       her body appears like a tulip —

yellow petals unfurl

       each particle of her being

feathering out

       as form begins to let go —

A constellation of leave-taking

       perhaps, but also

most accurately the self.

       Her pupils dilate into places

the others in the room

       don't yet go.

Vibration sugars the window- panes,

       Venetian blinds,

the cut-glass dime-store vase.

Not light, exactly,

      more a sublimation

like the moment of abeyance

      where the airplane lifts

            the air — the intermittent snow —

Art Lessons

And why does the light always disrobe
lightly from the left? The doorway
almost out of sight, the window
demurely vaulted? Someone has just left
the room or a servant's soon returning
with a letter yet unread. A samovar,
a sea chart, a novel by the daybed.
A lute sounds far away, a bell begins
to ring. The moment still can happen;
the singing only you could bring.

Transcendence

A summer wind clicks through the room
plastic curtains ecstatic as castanets.

Standing outside the rim of the body

you inhabit other lives —
Russian horses and red pigeon feathers —

weathered to beach glass, to scrim.

And this afternoon, as other Jews before,
you call out green syllables

nearly sing them:

incantation of salt air, ripened plum.

Anna Akhmatova wanders the halls
offering peppermints with dented spoons —

Under a different house of sky . . .

Praise humans that blunder us
into the great unknowing —

translate sea to transalpine
an epic fable to jazz-filled tulip field.

Cruise of the Christians

In March 1904, photographer Myra Albert Wiggins set sail from New York to Jerusalem to attend the World's Fourth Sunday School Convention.

All day you stroll around the ship
impatient as if at an exhibition;

you ride the wake and wobble
of the sea, you scrutinize the light-

rays splayed across the horizon,
the open circles of water-

fowl, curvature of cloud—
awaiting the unseen angle

of the cradle — a calling
out — perhaps religious —

or perhaps futile —
of elation, the wild

warp and weave of the
weather from Cairo to

Corfu — *Could you reconcile*
what was diaphanous there

with what was massive?
Aperture of phosphorescence

against the unreachable
eyes of the crew? By evening,

when the silver platters glide
away as if by God's own

hand; you return to the darkroom—
its known territory, dampish

and moss-laden to maneuver
light from pan to pan until

a wing appears, a zig-zag
of a woman's coat, then her

companion's — until all the passengers
rise from midnight prayers as if

cinematically on cue, as if
the God figure here is you.

Disappearing Trick

Photography was ideally suited for recording the problems of modern life.
—*for Myra*

White glass bowl of rose petals, fossil
of cedar and cypress leaf; small cryptogram of click —

release. I'll offer you hollyhocks, half moons,
small trays of shimmering bees; then scent the story

with Linden branches snipped from pocket parks
near your building. Cyano types, platinum prints, silver

gelatins — What compelled you toward such layers
of light, the interplay of softening and filtering?

On horseback, with hatchet, you caught mountaintops,
lilypads and bridges; then re-mixed the world

sampling New York and Oregon tinctures.
With cameras, glass plates, fine-boned

fingers, you crafted a husband, a child, a Sunday School
Cruise for Christians. Myra, is subject ever more than a handshake

of chaos and stillness? Old costume, fool-proof mask, small
plea of improvised resilience? Good-bye red snapper,

splintered clogs, dented pots of tea Out of the silt of a lifetime —
out of disappointment and out of fashion
                    —your own invisibility —

Song

At Middle-Life: A Romance

Let love be imminent and let it be a train;
let it arrive at dawn, its whistle whiskering the air —

all brightness and verb. Let it nearly race by
but not quite — this could be the story of your life.

Don't hesitate outside the dining car of eccentric
and dark-eyed strangers, contemplating their espresso —

ordering half the nerve. Let love be a breakfast
of crème cakes, pomegranate juice, a lively Spanish torte.

Love ambles its way through post-industrial towns,
past fields of alfalfa blooms, past poplars

that have always been there, though you've never
sensed their sacredness before. Let love be amazing.

And when the next station appears in full view —
all green tones and jazz tunes;

let two of these travelers disembark —
primed to begin their nights in pursuit.

Awaiting Further Instruction

This is the easy time — a cup of tea,
mandarins and chocolates.
Take a millennium and gaze
over the pine and periwinkle fence line.
Decipher the cat's song, the plane's thrum,
the soft moans of ink along paper.
Settle into the sofa with pillows, in book arbor;
this is you, forty-eight, the day after Thanksgiving.
The heat up, the rest of life not
yet beaten into hours, the next thought
still balanced on the ledge of something
new — like a doorframe — a place
for change — if only one could . . .
And here is the sky Novembered to a gauzy blue;
the Olympics flickering a northwest winter truth.
But what then? When come the afternoons
of arias; ascendance of the jasmine's creamy flowers?
The future self apprised of her red carpet entrance:
held up — postponed — appearing soon —

Entering the Abandoned Red Barn, Old Photograph

A periwinkle glimpse of sky, a pliant web
of walking and corn silk revealed

as we mark our way, honeycombed together,
revised by October stems and leaves;

satisfied with a walking stick, a condom,
and two mugs of cinnamon tea;

certain no one else had ever done what we would do —
create languorous love against

abandoned stacks of hay and watch
as the New England shifting clouds repeat,

repeat, repeat their message
love me, leave me, love me

as the dogs, Sasha and Yevo tongue
my palms, protest his ridiculously cunning knees.

And afterwards, after Sunday morning
news, and afternoon raspberry creams —

we wave good-bye — backpacks packed
thumbs angled out against the sky.

And I listen for the skeletal recalling
of our muscles, cartilage, and limbs:

yes, regrets, yes,
in louder, less extinguishable cries.

Day of the Disquieted Heart

February light filters the morning
        an amplitude of blue lengthening
                her body across the Sound.

Where do herons fly when they're alone?
        Does a bufflehead console itself
                with an open waterway?

In the prayer fields
        of invisible views, in this ferry crossing
                West Seattle — Vashon,

in overlooked islands and offices of clouds,
        a fog horn announces ourselves
                to ourselves —

our heart crack, mind break, wild crow cry why
        in the present sacred lifting
                and lowering —

water and stillness. Sky and grief.

Filter out ipod, cell phone, bride and groom.
        Here appears an interstate of wax wings,
                there, a rapacious ring of gulls.

Where is the edge of a wetland?
        How do we discern
                the crossed place on our boundary lines?

Is *come back* naked enough? *Accompany me.*

The crooked light
      of mourning follows me
            like a love knot beyond the body;

Would there still be searching
      if the found existed?
            Only the wound sings its own word.

The Lost

— *For Richard, 1977*

As *The Night of The Living Dead*
unreels before us in the dark
you whisper to me vignettes of film history
explain how the lost art of withdrawing
velvet curtains had anticipated
the moment before the action,
expressed the cinematic show.
How a person's hands had to be constant
eagerly holding down, arranging
one movement over the other
in a meditation that involved
the whole body.
And how after years of pulling the fabric
up and down
one old man in Tennessee is left
with an art no one else living
knows or wants to learn.
You bemoan how the arcing
of wrists has been replaced by automation
how tonight it's levers and cranks
which undress our classic screen.
This is the story of tragedy you tell me
while across the aisle people swallow ice
through plastic straws and tear into
gold-wrapped chocolate swans
oblivious to all we have lost.

The Never Born Comes of Age

All day you bubble into liquid pieces
like a bath's surface, like a showerhead
with its dial of tricks, its pulse.

All day you search for the baobab tree
and mangos, the day glow
lizards — the leper ladies

who laugh with you from empty bowls.

Remember Sa-a, his name
which meant *the lucky one*? How hours
hunched like logs no one could move,

time mugging the coffee table, the ledge

of each boys' elbows? You'd hear
the brag of the new Toyota,
your lover shouting *ina kwana,* calling out —

Remember? The millet fields,
the Nigerian make-up
girls used to bleach their skin,

your neighbor, multilingual and soccer-stricken?

Remember Prince and Freak Out,
the pink of washboard roads,
fast sex without a condom —

and its predictable results?

Little biscuit, lemon peel,
pig tether — the fetus
that quickly followed, never showed.

Here's the praise song to the almost
child, almost mother, father
— *almost, almost, almost* —

And voilá, Habiba, our caretaker

the day you left and didn't know —
the crush of her wise body like a
waterfall, a levy overflowed.

Loss streaming across cow dung and thistle —
And still here, beside the bath, this ghost-child,
dragging waterproof alphabet, soggy cupcake, silent whistle.

Refrain of the Woman
Who Has Lived Too Long Alone

Over the bed sheets, the single supper plate
absence of beloved, absence of self
absence of hunger on the bright kitchen shelves.

Absence of Cupids, of payphones, of Mars —
of girls pressed to boys who taste like fall rain —
absence riding a life switching trains.

Hello, absence, echoes through the wasteland
of night, *How are you keeping? What's new?*
Like a child checking the scent of her shoes.

It's a call and response, a checkpoint, a fugue —
Here, absence stars in the classic Film Noir
the banker's lamp burning by the empty boudoir.

.

After Watching A Sky
of Trumpeter Swans and Snow Geese

Today there's nothing but this embrace
of world —

a story's sun-dried sheets.

Today I'm thrown into
a sky of snow, in narrative
circles, white psalms.

Under fields empty of crops
and comfort; what holds us
here, enraptured —

klow wow, klow wow, klow wow?

May our desires rise
above like notes
from outdoor music halls.

May the tempo
hold like trumpeter swans
or snow geese — a forward

March formation, an aural sash
of silk and grace.
In other words,

let my pleadings be
a pleasure to hear; a
Morse code of small requests.

Attentive lover, cash to spare, another Northwest year.

Rental

I'm afraid to own a body, you said
the regressive tax on breast and thigh
would be too high; then you circled

my wrists, held them brightly
and I registered in your eyes, the look
I imagine of accountant or old paleontologist

appraising semiprecious finds.
When you pose me toward the light
and we touch, you take

a transparency with your eyes;
as if April evenings can be
known things, as if

our rental car agreement
extended to tongues and only then
under certain conditions

to wondrous singing.
Praise song for contracts signed
in pocket parks where we

descend with little savings — Bless
even the promissory note
reneged, the unreality of love's

retreating. Your voice remaining
a little distant, but still companionable
like the announcer on late night radio —

You Might Consider . . .

how my long life of losing men
could create a new international sport.

Men lost in the desert, men missing
in action from doorways and all night diners;

men making the most of fire
escapes, service stairs, the emergency aisle

of airplanes like *United.* Men
para-sailing after spaceship encounters.

I am accomplished in the world
of the see-you-later wave

as his pick-up truck disappears
traveling on to the next espresso stand.

Something in the curve of my collar,
the cut of my blouse sets them running.

They know they are in the hands of a master.
But when the coffee's on, the pumpernickel

toasted just right, I have to let them know;
I'm actually ready to let them go.

Curating My Death

I'm not afraid of dying, I just don't want to be there when it happens.
—— Woody Allen

Let me order my death as I would order a party

wrapped-up lightly in cornflower sacks —
Let me arrive at the all night caterer, exchanging

guitar riffs with Lou, scatting over and over, *may I help you?*

Prawn masala, cinnamon tarts, ginger ice cream and red plums.
Let the end come with spice, let the parting be sweet

as cheese blintzes raised to an oven-baked shrine.

May handsome musicians play bold Sevillanas,
Miles, Otis, The Supremes —

Bring in rounds of mourners, not afraid to dance

or celebrate butter cream and layered cakes —
a galaxy of frostings.

And after — we'll sip cups of Arabic coffee,

linger with lavender chocolate —
its own global paradise.

At the airport kiosk, I'll offer up last good-byes,

to acrobats and rabbis; landscape painters
and Mt. Rainier guides —

all the lives I intended to try.

Proceeding along the skyway, I'll find
a chair at Gate 2B, then check-in with the others;

in scintillant darkness we'll wait:
                    anticipatory, amiable, traveling free —

Doing Time

for my father

He liked to watch the light

of the clock face flicker on
his only indication

of the day
disappearing into night

5:00 P.M.
lit a pale-green moon

inside a room shrouded white.

*

He would count the hours
and the miles

from the time my plane touched
down to the second of arrival.

I'd offer him stories of the taxi man,

of a city called Seattle
where blueberry bushes keep

pace with wisteria vines.

*

The furthest west he ever traveled:

a cardiac chair by the bed,
the shower stall
in the distance

plastic tubes up his nose, down his throat.

☀

How to secure the word

write the weight
of a single second

inured in the not-
living, the not-dying —

infinite hospital evenings hopelessly endured.

Naming It

Shilshole: the shape in
which the estuary threads

her way inland to Puget Sound;

or ——to pull a thread
through the eye of a bead.

That same sense of direction —

staving off loss
by narrowing what we need.

Unexpected Song

Thank-you for sending me back
to the page, the open notebook,

El Duende's unfurled tail
along the table's edge.

Thank-you for apricot blossoms,
beach rose and blackberry vines;

that allow bright divinations
along the nearly-absent mind.

And hats off to the green
and white ferries over-riding

time-tables, taxes, spring tides;
to the brants' triumphant choir

casually premiering each April
along the waters of Beach Drive;

above Vashon, Bainbridge, Blake,
like a flyway to the heart.

Outside this raised window
lie early morning charms

traveling the air on blue lilac —
terrestrial and round:

the notes we are meant to sing
the possibility in each slight thing.

Chanterelle

Perhaps consider poetry
a gourmet grocery shop,

endless pyramids of
shape-shifting fruit:

persimmon, star flower, pomegranate —

and across the aisle
in hand-woven oval baskets:

Vietnamese coriander,
Thai basil, Chinese leaves.

Experiment without knowing
the exact region where

the pomegranate is grown
the pronunciation of the Chinese leaf.

But don't set out to deceive
the check-out girl;

you can't pretend that you're
a kumquat or a chanterelle.

And get away with it.

Instead, practice rapture —
and inquisitiveness, pose

a question to the golden
beet, the artichoke heart;

engage with a yellow fin.
The page relies

on the clean attempt
to move beyond the safe way.

Where is the ineffable?

Bring home a mango
muddle it with Kosher salt.

What the Grocer Knows

It's not their hunger that calls them here —
not the free range eggs, not the everyday

Christmas mandarins, not the pyramids
of potatoes: fingerlings and Peruvian blues;

not the marlin fillets, not the ahi steaks,

not the sound of jazz tunes drifting
above the gourmet frozen food.

They come for the patriotism of the cereal aisle —

colorful cartons calling out their names;
taste cheeses lined-up like small children:

asiago, machango, a drunken goat
spread from Spain.

Around the corner, the women

anoint their fists with *this week's* myth
calmly, as if in a darkened church

where candles flicker, then go.

Is this how we thought it best to live?
What words can we still follow?

At the check-out counter, under bags of edamame,
the grocer plants old finds: *Dreamscicles*

and mission figs. One common ball of twine.

The [In]Visible Architecture of Existence

Does the television console me? What about the microwave's
moon plate imprisoned in its cave, creating popcorn tarts

that ring a house-mix popping rhythm to the old cats singing?

Does the Bosnian clock eulogize the nightly cocktail hour —
a Blue Hawaiian by the beach, the bedroom mourn father's

lost fedora, misplaced with the rabbi — *a person of interest*

to Oregon police? Or perhaps, *Ye shall know us by*
our bathtub faucets, gooseneck silver spouts, sputtering forth

a cryptogram of birds against the patch-worked enamel —

What might they think, if indeed they could think —
the basement staircase kneeling in supplication to the rain

boots, brick-a-brac, squirrels? Surely, the crack in the linoleum

might show enlightenment — the imprint of our mass?
And when this season's aging model enters — uninvited —

with gammy skin and tiny beard — will she guild new narratives?

I listen to her step moving along the hyacinth stairs.
Is hers a wiser touch in the morning laundry air, the teacup lunch?

Soma cells divide, replace the body every year, but not

the water jug and window sashes — the oven-safe plastic ware.
The ghost self I will become turns fifty-one,

then seventy-four. Let her explore my world above

the bird's eye desk, Ptolemy's map, the book lined mess —
court it with the passion of a paramour.

Instinctively, may she attend this anthem —

this trick of bricks and glass, these gutters —
a covered heartland for our small claims rearranged.

Letter to the End of the Year

Lately, I am capable of small things.

Peeling an orange.
Drawing a bath.
Throwing the cat's tinsel ball.

Believe me, this is not unhappiness.

Only one question —
why this layering on of abeyance?

Though it is winter inside of me —

there is also spring and fall.

Yellow tulips in need of planting
root in a basket by the door.

Tonight, mortality seems cloistered in a pinecone

close-windowed, remote.

*What was the peak moment
of your happiness?*

And how did you know?

For weeks, it's been oatmeal,
the Internet, an Irish shawl.

I realize, I am growing older
and stranger.

     Please, don't misunderstand.

I am still impatient
still waiting for symbiant and swoon

     the litter of blue-gold —

          a one-time constellation:

Now, before you go.

Notes and Dedications

"Tulip Sutra" is for Mustafa and Reyyan Bal.

"Re-imagining My Life with Lions" and "In a Hospital Room in a City Where I Am Not" are in memory of Molly Daytz.

"An Army of Ellipses Traveling Over All She Does Not Say" is for Hodan Mohamud.

"Interview" and "Cereal Boxes" reference the Sarajevo Rose: the pattern made by a mortar shell exploding; specifically it refers to the imprint left on the tarmac.

"4 0' clock News @ House of Sky" is for Kelli Russell Agodon.

"Portrait with Lorca" borrows its last two lines from Lorca.

"What to Make of Such Beauty" is for Lejla Beslija.

"Transformation" is for Ilya Kaminsky.

"Aperture" is in memory of Abraham Morris Rich. The line "Each sadness needs a street name" is inspired by Olena Kalytiak Davis's line in "Mutilated Versions of Myself Write Poems, Treat Me with Irony and Condescension," *Each new loneliness needed a streetname.*

"Naming It": *Shishole* is a Duwamish word meaning "threading a needle" perhaps referring to the narrow opening in which Salmon Bay narrows into Shilshole Bay in Seattle, Washington.

"Interview" is for Larisa Kasumagic.

Myra Albert Wiggins (1869-1956) was born in Salem, Oregon; she was the first Northwest woman photographer to achieve high acclaim for her work and exhibit her pictures nationally and internationally in the company of Alfred Steiglitz and others.

The Myra Albert Wiggins poems owe a great debt to Carole Glauber whose book *The Witch of Kodakry The Photography of Myra Albert Wiggins 1869 - 1956*, published by Washington State University Press, informed and often jump-started the poems collected here concerning the photography, painting, and life of the artist.

"Hunger is the Best Cook, Homesickness; Paris Exposition, After Hours;" and "Polishing Brass" all take their titles from the photographs which inspired their writing. "A Corner of My Studio" and "Not a Still Life" take their titles from Wiggins' paintings. "Late Romance, Art Lessons, The Cruise of the Christians," "Mr. Myra Albert Wiggins Considers Their Arrangement," and "Disappearing Trick" all are attempts at imagining part of the trajectory of Wiggins' life story.

"Cruise of the Christians" borrows *Could you reconcile / what was diaphanous there with what was massive* from Seamus Heaney's "Lightenings," section x.

"The Lost" is for Richard Maxfield.

"Day of the Disquieted Heart" borrows inspiration from Charles Wright.

"After Watching a Sky of Trumpeter Swans and Snow Geese" is for Jan North.

"Unexpected Song" is for Peter Aaron.

"Letter to the End of the Year" borrows it's first line and general inspiration from "Postcard." published in *Her Soul Out of Nothing* by Olena Kalytiak Davis.

Susan Rich is the author of three collections of poetry, *The Cartographer's Tongue / Poems of the World*, *Cures Include Travel*, and *The Alchemist's Kitchen*. She has received the PEN West Poetry Award, The Times Literary Supplement Award, and the Peace Corps Writers Award. Her fellowships include an Artists Trust Fellowship from Washington State and a Fulbright Fellowship to South Africa. She serves on the boards of *Crab Creek Review*, Floating Bridge Press and Whit Press. Rich has received residencies from Hedgebrook, Ucross Foundation, and Fundacion Valparaiso. Recent poems have appeared in the *Antioch Review*, *Harvard Review*, *Poetry International* and *TriQuarterly*. Born in Brookline, Massachusetts, she now makes her home in Seattle, Washington, where she teaches English and Film Studies at Highline Community College.

Author photograph: Tom Collicott